This edition published in 1999 by Blitz Editions
an imprint of Bookmart Limited
Registered Number 2372865
trading as Bookmart Limited
Desford Road
Enderby
Leicester
LE9 5AD

Published and produced by ADC International - 1998 Eke Nazareth - Belgium
Printed in Dubai, 1999

"VAN GOOL'S"

Puss in Boots

Once upon a time in a village in a kingdom, there lived a miller and his three sons. The miller's family always had enough to eat, but none to spare. One day, the old miller was so sick that he called his sons to his bedside.

"I have no fortune," said the miller. "But you may share what little I have."

The miller's only belongings were his mill, his donkey and his cat. To his oldest son he left his mill, and to his middle son he left his donkey. To his youngest son, the miller left his cat. Then the old miller died.

While the youngest son was fond of the cat, he felt that his father had not dealt fairly with him, for his brothers could earn a living with a mill and a donkey, but it seemed that little fortune could be made with a cat. "I suppose you can catch mice," the young man said, scowling at the cat, "but what use is that?"

Suddenly, much to the young man's surprise, the cat spoke. "Look here," he said quite plainly. "Get me a fine hat, cape and boots, and I'll see that your fortune will be bright."

Astonished to hear the cat speak, the miller's son obeyed at once.

Taking his last coins, he went into the village and bought the clothes. The cat was very pleased when he slipped on the boots, hat and cape. Then he set off down the road, leaving his master to wonder if he'd been foolish to trust such an eccentric cat.

The cat, who soon came to be called Puss in Boots, stepped brightly along the road, until he came to a briar patch. There he lay down and pretended to be dead. Curious, a rabbit hopped out of the patch. Puss in Boots jumped up and seized it by the ears.

Puss in Boots marched directly to the king's palace, where he insisted on seeing the king at once.

Puss was escorted to the throne room, where he bowed deeply and presented the rabbit, saying, "Greetings, Your Majesty. My noble lord, the Marquis of Carabas, has sent me to deliver this gift to you personally, with special regards to the princess."

"Please give your master my thanks," said the king.

The next day Puss in Boots returned to the palace, presenting partridges to the king on behalf of his master. Again, the king was pleased with the gift. "The Marquis is a generous man," said the king.

Then, as Puss in Boots was leaving, he heard the king asking the princess if she was ready for their drive along the river.

Puss in Boots ran all the way back to his master, and instructed him to go at once to the river to bathe. When the young man questioned him, the cat said, "Trust me. Do as I say, and your future will be bright."

"Come now, hurry!" urged the cat. As they made their way to the river, Puss in Boots said, "Now, if anyone asks your name, tell them you are the Marquis of Carabas."

"Are you sure you know what you're doing?" asked the miller's son. Puss in Boots replied with a wink.

The young man took off his ragged clothes and left them on the riverbank. Then he dived into the river. "Ah! The water feels great, Puss. Are you coming in?"

Before the cat could reply, the royal carriage came rumbling past. "Help!" shouted Puss in Boots. "The Marquis of Carabas is drowning! Help!"

When the king heard the familiar name, he ordered that the young man be rescued. "Sire," the cat whispered to the king, so as not to embarrass the princess, "while my master was bathing, all his clothes were stolen."

Puss had cleverly hidden his master's clothes. The king ordered a servant to fetch one of his finest suits.

In no time, the young man was dressed in a royal outfit that made him look very handsome. “So you’re the Marquis of Carabas!” called the king.

“I’m privileged to meet Your Majesty,” replied the young man, bowing.

“Perhaps you’d like to join us for a ride in the country,” offered the king. The young man climbed into the royal carriage, and they set off.

Puss in Boots rushed down the road ahead of the carriage, until he came to a forest, where he found some woodcutters. “Listen here!” he shouted, brandishing his sword. “The royal carriage will be here shortly. When the king asks who owns these woods, you must tell him they are owned by the Marquis of Carabas, or you will be severely punished.”

Then Puss in Boots hurried farther down the road until he came to a large field that the peasants were reaping. "I am a royal messenger!" shouted the cat, as the peasants stopped to listen. "When the king passes by and asks who owns these fields, you must tell him they are owned by the Marquis of Carabas."

The peasants nodded agreement.

Soon, the royal party arrived and the king ordered the carriage to stop. "Who owns these fields?" he called to the peasants. Glancing nervously at the cat, the peasants replied, "The Marquis of Carabas owns all these fields."

"Well," said the king, "we've seen your vast forest, and now we see your fine fields."

The miller's son nodded, not knowing quite what to say. But the princess took his silence for modesty, and smiled.

Puss in Boots ran ahead of the carriage until he came to an enormous castle. The castle was owned by a dreaded ogre, who also owned all the land along the road. The cat trotted through the gate.

Upon his request, Puss in Boots was escorted to the ogre's chamber. "Pardon me," said the cat, removing his hat with a flourish. "I had to make your acquaintance, having heard tell of your fame far and wide."

The ogre was flattered, but replied gruffly, "I've no time for vanities. What is it you want?"

"I cannot believe stories that you can transform yourself into anything you want," said the cat.

"I shall prove I can do just that!" thundered the ogre. "And then you shall die for doubting my powers."

Before Puss in Boots could say another word, the ogre turned himself into a ferocious lion. The ogre's words dissolved into angry roars, as he waved his huge paw in the air, brandishing his sharp claws.

Puss was frightened nearly out of his boots. "If you please!" he shouted, to be heard above the roars. "That *is* amazing. But I doubt you could change yourself into something as small as, say, a mouse." No sooner had he spoken the words, then the vain ogre turned himself into a tiny fieldmouse. "Splendid!" cried Puss, clapping his paws together.

“And now I shall eat you!” cried the cat. As quick as a wink, Puss in Boots caught the mouse and ate him in one bite. Then he put on his hat, cleaned his whiskers, and made his way about the castle, sternly informing all the servants that they were soon to meet their new master.

Soon the royal carriage arrived, for the castle stood at the end of the road. Puss in Boots greeted the royal party at the gate. “Welcome to the castle of the Marquis of Carabas!” he exclaimed. “Perhaps you’d like some refreshment after your journey.”

The king was delighted that his new friend, of whom his daughter appeared to be very fond, lived in such a splendid castle.

"My house is your house," said the young man humbly.

The young man and the princess felt love growing between them as they gazed at each other. Holding hands, they walked dreamily up the castle steps with the king.

Puss in Boots smiled. "Catching mice can be of great use," the cat said to himself.

The group went into the Great Hall, where a cold banquet had been quickly prepared by order of the cat. The king proposed that the marquis marry his daughter, and the happy couple agreed.

A lavish wedding was planned for the marquis and the princess, who were so obviously in love. No one in the kingdom could doubt that it was a joyous event, for all the bells in the land rang out the good tidings. Lords and peasants alike were invited to the wedding, in which Puss in Boots played a part by proudly holding the princess's train.

At the wedding the new prince promised his brothers land and wealth. When they asked how he had come to such success, he winked and replied, "Great fortunes can be made with a cat."

As for Puss in Boots, he found the comforts of castle living to his liking, and he lived happily ever after.